Dances
With the Cranes
(poems on reincarnation)

Dances With the Cranes

(poems on reincarnation)

Brigadier G D Bakshi
SM, VSM

SHARADA

Sharada Publishing House
Delhi-110 035
2004

First Published : 2004

ISBN : 81-88934-17-8

SHARADA ₹ 500/-

Published by :
B.L. Bansal
SHARADA PUBLISHING HOUSE
(Publishers on India's Past and Present)
2094/165, Ganeshpura, Tri Nagar
Delhi-110035, India
Ph. : 011-30921560, 27552102
Email : bansal_spn @ indiatimes.com

Laser Typesetting by :
Creative Graphics
Ph. 55290641

Printed at :
Santosh Offset, Delhi

Dedicated
to
His Holiness
The Dalai Lama
of Tibet
and
to my teacher
Lama Thin Le Dorji
a Lama of the Ying-Ma-Pa sect

CONTENTS

FOREWORD

Poets like Brigadier Bakshi appear once in an age. He is a great sage and saint and truly spiritual in his sweep.

His poetry is not just a poetry for the nonce, few verses to delight masses, few poems to be read and cast off, but they must be read and read again and again to reach the TRUTH he has treasured in each verse.

Dances With The Cranes - as the poet himself writes, celebrates the magic and mystery of Rebirth that these birds personify in their migration and passage.

Standing on the top of a lonely mountain, the poet shrieks:

"Who am I?
Who was I?
Why do I remember the past?"

He shivers. The majestic Black cranes seem to be the very incarnation of Death and the mystery of our Rebirth.

Each year these magnificent cranes descend on the slopes of Bhutan. They sail like ghostly apparitions and fill the air with their shrieks. Then they are gone again on their migration to distant lands and tranquil marshes.

The poet once climbed a mountain and after descending came to a monastry. Its strange mysterious perfume made him giddy and faint. Later, the poet's Tibetan Teacher told him that he had lived many lives and in one he was a Buddhist monk.

These gorgeous Cranes with Red beaks, Red breasts and enormous Black wings, come from life to life in our dreams. Their vision has touched the core of the poets being and reached across the aeons of time - to distant times in distant lives under different suns and distant shores.

They remind us of the restlessness of things, of beginnings and endings, of golden dawns, noon suns and endings ending in beginnings. They remind him of flashes and visions that rise like sparks of a distant fire that has consumed so many lives.

The poet says that the learned Lama droned a chant that cast a spell on the clouds so that they burst into torrential rains.

The priests from the pyramids have traced the flight of the soul to its beginning.

And very pensively the poet cries

"Birds migrate
The self transmigrates
It flies from life to life
Sparks migrate from pyre to pyre".

He continues thus

"The Tao Te Ching
stresses the interconnectedness
of all things
Everything, every being is
In communication with all vital things
The Cosmic web weaves on
A strand of Unity
In all the bewildering
multitudes of being".

The poet solemnly ends thus

"I am not really free
I read the
The Tibetan Book of the Dead
The Bardo Thodal
will set me free".

All those vexed with the mysterious march of events in every day ness - craving for liberation from mortal coil- can get solace in the poets poems. They must be read with earnestness, belief and resolve to be free from birth.

It is a most arduous task, those bent to achieve liberation in this life itself, can contact the poet himself and be blessed.

Krishna Srinivas
President World Poetry
Society and Editor
'Poet' Magazine

PROLOGUE

Poems on Reincarnation

The central theme of this collection of poems is "Reincarnation". The best liet motif of Reincarnation, of the transmigration of the soul, is the seasonal migration of birds. The one bird that best ensouls this theme of transmigration is the Swan. The other is the majestic Black winged Crane – (the national bird of Bhutan). It is a magnificent bird – huge and arresting in form. It has Black wings, with blood Red beak and neck and splashes of Red on its breast. The juxtaposition of black and red make it an apt symbol of death and rebirth. Each year, starting sometimes as early as August or September, these magnificent cranes migrate from the marsh lands of the River Leena and Ob in Siberia and from Ladakh, Tibet and China to the lower slopes of the Bhutanese Himalayas. The Bhutanese call them "Thrung Thrung Kam". Some 300 or more sail into the marshes of Phobijkha (or Wangdi) in Western Bhutan and Bomdeling (or Tashi Yangtse) in Eastern Bhutan. Some of them fly down to the Sangti valley in the western Kameng district of Arunachal Pradesh. They sail in like ghostly apparitions and fill the maize fields with their clamour. Then they are gone again on their migration to distant lands and tranquil marshes in the spring.

In Chinese and Japanese art forms, the Black winged crane is a very familiar motif. A thousand black winged cranes descending upon the lake are the most apt metaphor for the transmigration of the human spirit.

These poems are inspired by the majesty of these magnificent birds. I could think of no better metaphor for reincarnation than these Black winged, Red breasted cranes that migrate each year to Bhutan. "Dances with the Cranes", celebrates the magic and mystery of rebirth that these birds personify in their migration.

Many, many years ago, I had a very strange experience of déjà vu. I was walking alone in a lonely field when a strange, acrid incense burst upon my nostrils. I will never forget that acrid burning smell and the faint hint of a lingering perfume it carried. It came suddenly from no where as it were. There was not a human habitation or a fire in sight. I was amazed and overwhelmed. The perfume seemed to assail all my senses at once. It was so real.

Some years later when I first went to the house of my Tibetan teacher – the Ying Mapa Lama Thin Le Dorjey, I suddenly breathed that acrid incense again. No, he had not lit it in his house. He could not smell it either. It came from a deeply buried layer of the self, a long forgotten memory of a different life and an association with things Tibetan. I was haunted by the acrid strangeness of that unetherial perfume. I smelt it again, whenever I encountered any Tibetan household or any Tibetan artefact or carpet. In a strange way that deeply buried memory trace would surface again and fill me with a restlessness and vague yearnings.

I solved the mystery at long last. I was on a patrol to a very remote area in North Sikkim. We had gone on the approaches to the sacred Kangchendzonga mountain. We climbed the 16,000 feet high Kishong La Pass. Then we descended steeply and came to the Toloung Gompa. We camped there for the night. It is a remote and secluded monastery. The skull of the Third Chogyal of Sikkim is kept embalmed in gold at this shrine. We were tired and fell into a deep stupor. When I got up the next morning and came out of my snow tent – my nostrils were assailed by that sharp, acrid scent. This time it came from a real, physical source. It came from the alter of the monastery. I ran inside, breathless with excitement. There, before the alter of the deity, the monks were burning some leaves in a Copper Urn. The burning leaves gave off an acrid smoke and lingering on that smoke was that faint, mysterious perfume. I shivered violently from head to foot. I spoke to the Sikkimese monks. The leaves were of the stunted Rhododendron bush that grows on the higher slopes of the Himalayas. When burnt it gives a faint, lingering perfume superimposed upon that acrid, burning smell.

How did I know this pungent perfume ? I do not know. My Tibetan teacher said that perhaps many lives ago I had been a Tibetan monk. A different me had inhaled that acrid perfume. Many lives ago a monk had breathed that magic scent of solemnity. Every time I saw something Tibetan – some motif or a carpet or rug, some Copper kettle or Urn with Dragon motifs – some deep association would trigger off that strange experience of Déjà vu in the form of the memory of a perfume. I have been here before. I have breathed that incense earlier.

A Tulku, an incarnate Lama is asked to recognise his rosary, his monks bowl, his Russet Red robes and personal artefacts. A plain humble monk recognises a strange perfume from a very distant niche in space and time.

I have stood on lonely mountain passes and seen the 'Darchens', the prayer flags snap-snapping in the breeze. I have suddenly been overwhelmed by a strange restlessness – by a desire to scream at the nameless void. "Who am I ?" "Who was I ?" "Why do I remember these things ?" The answer is a deep silence. Only the sound of the 'Darchens'–the flags snap – snapping in the breeze and a faint acrid incense. I shiver. The majestic Black Cranes now seem the very incarnation of death and the mystery of our rebirth. There is a riddle there some where, waiting to be unravelled and solved. Only, I do not know what the questions were in the first place. Death is like that. So is sleep and so is Rebirth.

When we dance with the Black Winged Cranes possibly we will understand, for like the ancient Shamans, we would have lived out that metaphor in our dance.

G D Bakshi
Brigadier

DRAGON KINGDOM

In the Dragon
Kingdom
of the serpent slayer
gorgeous cranes
with red beaks
red breasts and enormous
Black wings appear
They came year
after year
to our valley
in the Hermit kingdom
even as they come
from life to life
in our dreams.

20

BLACK CRANES

The black cranes have
come
Mother I saw them sail
over the Gedung
Monastery, majestically
glide past the peaks
into our valley
and the rocks
rang out
to their liquid
cries
The vision that
filled my eyes
touched the core
of my being
and reached
across the aeons
to the distant times

when I had
heard the same cries
perchance so
many lives before
under a distant Sun
on a distant shore
The lyrical cries of the cranes
have touched the
deepest strings
of my soul
as they sailed
across the craggy
snow peaks
and alighted
in the Maize
fields to root
for tubers rare.

DANCES WITH THE CRANES

Hear them mother
The cranes are crying
The flowers have
withered
the leaves are dying
they have cut
the golden corn
The fields of Maize
and rice
are bare
and there
look there,
his form
is dancing
with the cranes
prancing to their
songs
and outstretched wings
Black wings of death
blood Red breasts and beaks.
He belongs now
To the dark wings
of death.

SONGS OF LIFE

Yet his songs
are of life
of this life
and that life
of an "isness"
that is forever
of a "suchness"
of things
that the
Tao Te Ching
Illumines.

FOREVER AMBER

Sometimes
The Black Cranes
frighten me
mother
for they come
year after year
with an unfailing
relentlessness of
things
of beginnings
and endings
of golden dawns
and majestic dreams
of high noon Suns
and strange endings
that end in
more beginnings
Cyclical
inexorable
forever
Amber.

MEMORIES AND MOON BEAMS

The Amber
and Amyhest
the Turquoise and Jasper and Jade
and Coral
the Lapis Lazuli, the Cats eye
the steaming Momos,
the meat dumplings
the noodles and
tender green
shoots of bamboo fronds
The red chop sticks, Fooyongs
the mush rooms
and fungi and sonorous songs
meals made of moon dust
and the pale
ambience of
many moon beams
Memories
and voices
with no sound
sail upon the
black wings of
these mountain Cranes.

REINCARNATION

The beads
of the rosary
are counted again
the prayer wheel
once more
is Twirled around
the prayers rise
like foam
to heaven
they have no meaning
and they have no sound
what are the words
where are the symbols
what is the meaning
of my dreams ?

RUSSET RED ROBES AND ROSARIES

Why do I
remember ?
Why do these
flashes and visions
arise
like the sparks of
a distant fire
that has consumed
so many limbs
Why do I remember
that faint incense
that russet red
robe
Where did I feel
that rosary before ?
Mother
I shiver
I fear
the inexorable
nature of things.

BEGINNINGS AND ENDINGS

Do all beginnings
end in endings
that are but
beginnings of other things ?
What is the
true nature
of things
that were
there then
but are not
here
anymore
Do all birds
sing but
once to the
full moon
or is it the
tune
that waxes and wanes
there, then and here
again
and again ?

I DO NOT KNOW

I do not know
but I saw
the cranes
go – last year
I saw them
fly away.
They had sailed
off their rocky
perch
grazed past the
leaves of Acacia
and Birch
on jet Black wings.
Their cries had
sailed through
the valley green
and a shiver had
run down my being.

THE CRANES COME AGAIN

This year
they are here
again
they floated down
one day
like a dream
apparation
on ghostly wings
snowy white
cranes
with red beaks
red breasts
and enormous
black wings
Is there
a lesson there
my dear
on the eternal
"isness"
of all things.

I HAVE HEARD THAT SONG BEFORE

I have heard
that song
before.
I knew it
then.
I do not sing
it anymore.
For he who
sang this
song then
did not
look like me
before
I dreamt
of him
Yet when I
heard the
Herons cry
I knew in a flash
upon the inward eye
that he was I
and I was he
in the "suchness" of things.

IMAGININGS

Why do I cry
when I hear
the Herons cry ?
Why do I shiver
when the Black Cranes
outstretch their wings ?
Their siren
song echoes
and re-echoes
in the hills.
I saw the things
they gave me to
see again
to see
if I remembered
the true suchness
of things
or was the
crying Crane
a Shamans
dream ?
Nothing
but an apparation.
Nothing
but my imaginings ?

BLACK CRANES COME YEAR AFTER YEAR

The Black Cranes
my dear
come year
after year
such is the
nature of things.
They were here
last year
they are here
again
Do you hear
their cries
Do you see
their eyes,
their enormous
Black wings
do you see
their beaks
that are so red
Do you see
the corpse
that is dead?

STRANGE PLUMAGE

The strange plumage
of a strange bird
that strange song
that haunting dirge
the floating cries
upon the breeze.
My eyes scan
the voids
of the heavens
I throw the
grains of white
rice
as an offering
to the breeze
to take it to
those I can
not see anymore.

THE BLACK CRANE COMES

The Black Crane
comes
he comes, comes
evercomes !
He overcomes
the illusory
nature of
things.
The serpent
is not the
rope
the Pink Heron
does not sing
of the inexorable
ending of all
beginnings.
His graceful flight
is not a dream.
This stream
does not arise
here
It comes from afar
It has taken to wing
from a distant shore.

HERONS SONG

Sing, Sing
the Herons song
he belongs
to a niche
in time
that we do not know
it was not then
nor is yet to come.
It is now
for ever more.
He sings
songs
that come
to our ears
year after year
the numberless
days slip past
the song remains
as it was
in the beginning.

TRUTH

Or does it ever begin
and does it ever
have an ending ?
How can something
end that
never in truth
had a beginning ?

REGAL WINGS

The Blacks Cranes
have spread
their regal wings.
They are flying.
Look to the branches
bare my son
their leaves are dying.
The trees are bereft
and bare
and we
are crying.
You and I
we sat on the mountain tops.
Sang the songs
that the black cranes
had brought to us
from the marsh lands
of the rivers Leena and Ob.
Today as they wheel
upto the Sun
in spirals
of prayer.
The trees again are bereft and bare
and we
are crying
for a part of us
is dying
once more.

A "NOW" FOREVER

The Stags in the mountain
The crags on the "Ri"
The Black Antelope
and the Herons free.
The Red breasted Cranes
with their regal wings
the snowy white Storks
and the Purple Moorhens
sing
songs that never
began in time.
Therefore there can
be no endings
to this golden time
It will ever be
a beginning
a "Now"
that is forever.

I LOVE YOU MOTHER

I love you
mother
for ever more
you have
been to me
my mother
my beginning
in the womb
of time
The poems
that we have sung
together
have been
bequeathed to us
by the aeons.

BUDDHA PURNIMA

Purnima
the light
of the
enlightened one.
I saw the
world draped
in your
silver ambience
and I saw
a shadow
sail across
the face
of the moon
A Black crane,
it was flying
Even as I
was crying
in the lap
of my mother.

WE LIVE EVEN AS WE DIE

We live
even as we die
in our
beginning.
To our poem
there was
no point of
origin.
Our poem thus
has no ending.
The wave
that sank before
has risen
again.
I heard
a new born babe
wailing
in the
evening.
His beginning
was the days
ending.

LEARNED LAMA

The learned
Lama
droned a chant
he cast a spell
on the clouds
so they arose
in billows
then it rained
and lightening lit the sky
I have seen faces
in the mirror
that were not
mine
yet they were me !

CAN THE 'I' EVER DIE

Can the 'I'
ever die
The eye
of the beholder
gazed on
unseen.
Aye !
The 'I' in us
can never die
It never did
have a beginning
why speak then
of endings ?

NAMELESS YEARNINGS

She walked
with me
when I was
young
She held my
hand
and it was
warm
sunshine
to see
the love
in her eyes
and the
gentleness
in her gaze.
The breeze
is full of
sighs
and vague
feelings and
nameless yearnings.

SONGS THAT SOB ON THE BREEZE

So many books
of Poems
So many voices sing
songs that
sob on the breeze.
Songs that whisper
through the Juniper trees.
Songs that bob and
sparkle in the
sunshine.
Songs that rush
through the
wings
of those regal
Hermit cranes.

MOTHER I MISS YOU

Mother
I think of you
and sometimes
I start crying
may be I miss you.
The utter loneliness
of being unloved
is terrifying.

UGLINESS

Were we born
to ugliness ?
You and I ?
So that we
would be
a burden
unto ourselves.
So that we would
sigh with relief
when we die.
Do not cry.
Look there.
In the light
that lights
the line
where the earth
meets the sky
we will meet
those who have
loved us forever
despite our ugliness.
We will meet
those who know
the inner harmony
of our beings.

COMPASSION

Compassion
is a many
splendoured
thing.
I remember
the compassion
in those eyes
The clouds weep
the wind sighs
through the Maize
fields
and suddenly like a
clarion call
from another sphere
I hear
The Black cranes
cry.

KING OF CRANES

He sails in,
the leading one.
His black wings
shining in the Sun
His red breast
breasting the
mountain breeze
with graceful ease
he alights upon
the fields of golden
corn.
His long legs
steady his sweeping
glide.
In long
and easy strides.
The king of the
Black cranes
has come.

CLAMOUR OF THE CRANES

And then
the clamour
of the cranes
fills the skies
Their constant
caws and
liquid cries
rise like a
chant from the
winged
minstrels
of heaven.

MIGRATORY BIRDS

The Pink Herons
are here
in their hundreds.
The Purple Moorhens
from the vale
glow with a Red luminiscence
The whistling Teals
rise in swarms
from the lake waters
and fly in Graceful
"Vees"
The Grey lag Geese
have come from
the Siberian Plains
The Pintails
and Jet black Coots
and Cormorants
have come again
The Snake bird is
drying its wings.

THE BIRDS

The whistling Teals
and Greylag Geese
all these
the Jacanas
and Spoon bills
The Black necked Crane
and Grey Heron
The cries of the Sibis
and the snowy white cranes.
The Peacocks with regal mein.
The boat glides on
the reed margins
of the marsh.
The harsh frost of
the winter chill.
the dappled sun shine
thru the feligree of leaves,
the trellis works
of ideas
floats on nameless dreams
and unspoken yearnings.

THE KING FISHER

The King Fisher hovers
above the pool
then darts in
a flash of Brown
and Turquoise Blue.
The Green Parakeets cry
in droves
and rise like a cloud
from the trees
The gaggle of Geese
the chicks and coots
the Bamboo fronds
and tender shoots and
the Green Pigeons
cooing their Green
ambience.
At dawn I heard
a Coucals cry
"Coup – Coup"
the sound rose to the sky
until – the sudden
flutter of wings
Now no bird sings
and silence
reigns once more
in the marsh.

SACRED IBIS

The sacred Ibis
raises its curved beak
It flew from amidst the
Papaya reeds
on the margin of
the Nile.
The Egyptian Eagle
has spread its
regal wings
The painted storks
and Grey Herons
have all sailed in
The seasonal rites of
passage are on
The Priests from the Pyramids
have traced the flight
of the soul to its beginning.

BIRDS MIGRATES THE SELF TRANSMIGRATES

Birds Migrate.
The self
transmigrates.
It spreads
its invisible
wings
and flies from
life to life
The sparks
migrate
from
pyre to pyre.
In desire
life has its
beginnings.
It ends in
the funeral fire
and the self
takes to wing.

INCENSE

In the Gompa
the Lamas intone
their baritone
chants and sing
their sonorous songs.
The butter lamps
flicker in the gloom.
The acrid incense
of the rhododendrons
burning in the metal pans.
Their memory lingers on
from life to life
The scent that
burst upon my
nostrils in the
Monastery
in a flash
illumined the
mystery of
Who I was
and who I am.

RIMPOCHE

That child
had such
grave eyes
and solemn mein
He is
an incarnation
a Tulku
of the Rimpoche
the most precious
one who has come again
his mortal remains
are resting
in that white
Chorten
in the middle of that
stark and barren plain.

IRON MOUNTAIN

When they
took him
to the golden
roofed Gompa
on the Iron Mountain
The child
Lama
clung to
the finger
of his mother
I think
I saw him
crying, He
used to stand
in the fields
and watch
The Black Cranes
Flying
Now he will stand alone
and intone
The Tibetan Book
of the Dead and Dying.

DANCES WITH THE CRANES

I have come again
to dance
with the Black
Necked Cranes
See for me
they have outstretched
their regal wings
Their cries ring
in the emptiness
Their strident songs
echo from the hills
where I belong.

I CHING

Go bring
the I Ching.
Let us devine
the shape of
things
yet to come,
The course of lives
not yet begun.
We will discern
who you were
and what you are
to become.

TAO TE CHING

The Tao Te Ching
deals with the
interconnectedness
of all things.
Everything
every being
is forever
in communion
with all other things.
The cosmic web
weaves on
a strand of unity
in all the
bewildering
multitudes of
being.

TWO GOLDEN OREOLES

Two Golden Oreoles
sat on the
branches of
the Akṣhay Vat
The deathless tree.
One sat and
pecked
upon the fruit,
the other was free.
Its gaze fixed
at eternity
it looked on
impassively
at the bird
that revelled
in the fruit of
the Tree.
One bird was free
from the cycle of births
The other returned
again and again
to the Tree.

WISDOM OF THE ASHWATHA TREE

The Akshay Vat
The Ashwatha
Tree
of Eternity
has spread its
roots into the sky
and its branches
deep in the
bosom of the
earth
A metaphor of
creation, the cosmic birth
its wisdom
frees us
from the cycle
of becomings.

BARDO – THE BOOK OF THE DEAD

Mother you left
me at the golden
gates
of the monastery
From here I can not see
The Maize fields of
my land of birth
I miss the Green
trees of my valley
I can not hold your
hand and see
the dances of
the Back necked
cranes
I wish I could see
my little friends again
Here I can not laugh
or clap my hands
I'm not really free as yet
I read the Tibetan
Book of the Dead
The Bardo Thodal
will set me free.

GELUNG TRUMPHETS

The huge
Gelung Trumphets
echo in
the gloom
of the valley.
Their wail
sobs upon
the plain
like the sound
of a dragon
in mortal pain.
The fire flies
glimmer
in the night
I shiver with
fright and
huddle
closer to the
roasary
you gave me

WILL YOU RECOGNISE ME ?

In another
birth
In another life
perhaps
they will ask me
to recognise
the roasary
you gave me
but I feel lonesome
and alone.
This Monastery
is really not
my home.
From here
I can not see
the Black necked
Cranes
dancing so gracefully
in the fields of
our home.
Sometimes again
beyond the sweep
of human
memory

68

I will recognise
your roasary
but mother
will you
recognise me ?

OM MANE PADME HUM

Hail
To the Jewelline
luminosity
of our
immortal minds !
The ties that
bind
me to the
walls of
this monastery
have melted
away in tears
Do you see
I am free again
as I was
in the
beginning.

OM A HUM

Om
A hum
Bum
Guru
Padmasambhav
Hum!
Come rain
and thunder
Hum
Let lightening
light the sky
and open
that third eye
a inner
illumination.
Hum!

WHIRLPOOLS IN THE RIVER OF TIME

What are we
you ask?
We are whirlpools
in the river
of time.
The water in us
the matter in us
flows on free
in the river
of time.
Yet our forms
remain constant
and adamantine.
Like whirlpools
in the river
of time.

FRAGMENTS OF ETERNITY

In the afternoons
when the sonorous
snores of the monks
float upon the air
of siesta time
I stay up alone
and stare
into the vacancy
of space and time.
I ask myself
who am I ?
What will become
of me
when I die ?
Will I forever
cease to be
or shall
the fragment of eternity
that was me
return to eternity
again ?

RIVERS FLOW

Rivers flow.
Trees grow.
Flowers bloom
and fade.
the light and shade.
the tapestry of time
is woven from
our dreams.
In that deathless
Stream.
The ripples eddy
and bob
on the
River of time.
We are whirlpools
that are formed
and unformed
in the flow.
They appear now here
they vanish and go.
The same form appears
downstream
in another space
and another time.
The River of time
flows on forever.

WHO AM I YOU ASK?

Who am I ?
You ask ?
And I reply
why, indeed
why.
Should we wrestle
with our thoughts
Those who wish
to learn
should take up
the urn
and go again
to that barren plain
and meditate upon
the Blueness of the sky.

THAT TRUTH IS NOT TAUGHT

That truth is
not taught
That truth is not
wrought
by mere thought
The truth
lies within
In stillness
In the utter
silence of
"Shunyata"
you may hear
the song
of the River of Time.

THE RIVER OF HAPPINESS

The Ky Ling Chu
is the river
of happiness.
It wells up
in the aridness
of our hearts
when we –
transcend thoughts.
It makes us
cry
with the happiness
of a deep
understanding.

WAVES IN THE SEA

We are waves
in the sea
of the heart.
In the
"Hridyat Samudrat"
we rise as waves
of joy
we enjoy pure bliss.
Our beings are
boundless
we are not that
nor this.
Our forms are eternal
like whirlpools
in the river of time .
Their whirling forms
a vortex of form
that vanishes
from sight
but to our delight
It reappears again
down the line
In the river of
space and time

That very form
that we saw then
has reappeared
in another time.

MYSTERY OF THE MAGIC LAKE

I have heard again
the Herons cry
I have seen once more
the Black Cranes fly
over the magic lake.
That mystery
has only deepened
with the years.
I do not shed any tears
anymore
for those who have gone.
The vortices
of the whirlpools
of their form
will come again
down the line
In the ever flowing
River of time.

HERONS CRY

Herons cry
"we do not die"
The Black winged
Cranes
outstretch their wings
and dance
the dance of death.
Our breath is merged
with the eternal breath
of the universe
our minds with the Cosmic Mind
Lead us then
from darkness
to light
From death
to eternity
From untruth
to that shining truth!

WE WILL COME AGAIN

We shall come again
In a different space
and another time.
The white Chorten
of sadness
in that plain sublime
is a mere monument
to myself
and time.

DO NOT CRY

Do not cry
For I was he
and he was I.
The one whose
mortal remains
are embalmed
in that Chorten
in that vast
and barren plain
has come again
to form
another whirlpool
in the river of time.

DEATH ON THE BATTLEFIELD

Do you know
How many times
Have we died before?
Sometimes I see
visions
of bloody battlefields
so full of gore
I see the slashing swords
The flashing spears
That glisten
I listen
And I hear
The terrifying screams
Of the stricken
And the dying
I hear them crying
I cringe as I feel again
The pain
Of steel tearing through
My flesh and bone
I see again
That spray
Of droplets of blood
Flying in the air

Suddenly it becomes so silent
And still
My battered body falls
In the field
But I feel myself freed
Of my mortal coil.
I stand alone in the tumult
And see
My own cast off coil below.

CHERRY BLOSSOMS

I am now
A sunkissed
Fountain of joy
I am a whirlpool
In the river of time
I go for now
I vanish
Without a trace
But that form
That face
Will reappear again
As one more whirlpool
Down the line
In the ever flowing river of time
We will marvel again
Over the exquisite perfection
Of a Cherry Blossom
In spring time

EPILOGUE

The central leitmotif of these poems is the Black Necked Crane *(Grus Nigricollis).* From September to December each year, these cranes migrate from Ladakh, Tibet and the colder regions of China to Eastern and Western Bhutan and the Western Kameng division in Arunachal Pradesh. These cranes live in pairs and are known for their lifelong conjugal devotion. They are called *"T hrung thrung kam"* in Bhutan and *"T hrung thrung karmuk"* in Arunachal Pradesh. These birds are considered harbingers of good fortune and are deemed as good omens. Today these birds are an endangered species. There are just 300 of them left in the whole of Bhutan. Will these magnificent birds die out forever? It is my fervent prayer and forlorn hope that these poems will perchance generate an awareness about these magnificent birds. An awareness that will help us to save these harbringers of good fortune from extinction. The *T hrung thrung kams* do not deserve to die. They symbolise hope and their red beaks and black wings are symbols of resurruction and reincarnation. These birds will never die. They will never cease to be. They will remain till eternity, symbols of life and symbols of hope. May the marshlands of Wangdi and Bomdeling never be bereft of their songs and the lakes of the Sangti and Tso-kar resonate forever to the dances with the cranes.